Poet Fishing

Colin Shakespeare

First published in 2005
By Oak Press (Bradford) Ltd.
113 Station Lane
Bradford
BD11 2BX

All rights reserved
Copyright ©Colin Shakespeare 1983, 1985, 1988, 1994, 2005

Colin Shakespeare is hereby identified as author of this work in accordance with Section 77 of the Copyright, Designs and Patents Act 1988

ISBN 0-95091-675-7

This book is sold subject to the condition that it shall not by way of trade or otherwise, be lent, resold, hired out or otherwise circulated without the publisher's prior consent in writing in any form of binding or cover other than that in which it it published and without a similar condition including this condition being imposed on the subsequent purchaser.

Printed by: The Amadeus Press, Cleckheaton, West Yorkshire, BD19 4TQ.

Poet Fishing

New and Selected Poems
1983-2005

OAK PRESS (Bradford) LTD

For Barbara and John and Julie

Colin Shakespeare was born in Pontefract, West Yorkshire, in 1929. He was educated at Hemsworth Grammar School and in 1950 he qualified as a pharmacist from Bradford Technical College. He worked as a community pharmacist and from 1970 he had his own pharmacy in Bradford until he retired in 1995.

By the same author
Seamers (1983)
Spinning (1985)
The FIve Seasons (1988)
To Be a Condom & other Poems (1994)
22 Cricket Poems (1996)

All published by OAK PRESS (Bradford) Ltd.

8 of the cricket poems – Cricket Calendar; Sonny Ramadhin; To Sir Len Hutton; Frank Tyson at Sydney; Brian Close; England v Australia, Headingley, 1981, Tribute to Ian Botham; Mike Brearley and The Umpire appear in the 2004 MCC anthology of cricket verse, A BREATHLESS HUSH.

POET FISHING won the Bradford Libraries' poem of the month competition in April 1996.

Contents

FROM SEAMERS (1983)

Grandfather 9
The Village 10-11
Underground 12
Catland 13
Roll Call 14
Assembly Line 15
The Gunmen 16
The Meths' Drinker.. 17
Jack and Jill 18
Bumble-Bee 18
1939 19
Hiroshima 19
As My Father Lay Dying... 20-24
To Absent Friends... 25

FROM SPINNING (1985)

Gina.. 26
Spinning... 27
The Skylark 28
Miner With Silicosis 29
At The Head-Butting Ball 30
Idling Speed 31

FROM THE FIVE SEASONS (1988)

Body Chemistry 31
Cricket Grass-Widow 32
For You 33
Weathers 34-35

Contents

Dry-Stone Walling	36
Habits	37
To Stanley Horner	38-41

FROM TO BE A CONDOM & OTHER POEMS (1994)

Man's Best Friend	42
The Double Glazier's Love Song	42
Poet Fishing	43
Pit Closures	44
Golfer – Fred Beaumont	45
Snapdragon	46
To Be A Condom	47
A Russian Blue Cat	48
Bottle Bank	49
Song Of The Air	50

NEW POEMS

Summer Hummer	51
Air	52
Mortgaged	53
Love Song	54
Bearings	55
Scholarship Lads	56

FROM 22 CRICKET POEMS (1996)

Cricket Comes	57
Cricket Calypso	58-59
Sonny Ramadhin	60
To Sir Len Hutton	61
J. H. Wardle	62

Contents

Openers	63
Tribute To Ian Botham	64
F. S. Trueman	65
Joel Garner	66
Viv Richards	67
Making A Cricket Bat	68-69
Keith Miller	70
The Umpire	71
Elegy For Jim Laker	72
Brian Statham	73
Garry Sobers	74-75
Frank Tyson At Sydney, 1954	76
Brian Close	77
Jamaica, Jamaica	78-83
England v West Indies 1988	84
Mike Brearley	85
Death Of John Arlott	86

NEW POEMS

Cricket At Upton	87
Cricket Calendar	88-90
Freddie Flintoff	91
A Prayer For Cricketers	92
Millennium Hymn & Tune	93-95

Grandfather

Grandfather, toothless and stubble, loved lettuce, would
Roll leaves into a cigar, then finely shred
With a knife and each shred take up
On the perilous journey to his mouth
As his hands shook and shook and shook.
Always it was like this; bread he took
Dipped in tea and tea from a half-filled cup.

Each summer he came to stay, sat straw-hatted
In the sun, each day read the Bible that fitted
The waistcoat pocket where his heart was;
Kneeling, he'd cut the lawn meticulously
With scissors: no grass received more courtesy.

He went to bed early and sometimes in the night
We'd wake to hear him singing lustily
Fight the good fight with all thy might.

He lived to a good age until his legs filled with water.
Married twice, he procreated sixteen children.
My mother was his favourite daughter.

The Village

My father, brothers, went down,
Down, down the mine,
The nearest I got
Was to the cage side.

Two steel rods slugged with grease,
A wire rope held the cage;
'Come on in,' they said, 'come on.'
'It's only half a mile down.'

When they came back
They were black, black as coal is black.
Back home they talked pit talk.
I could only sit and listen.

The village was the pit
And the pit was the village,
Only one bus an hour
And where did it go to?

They played nipsy, pitch-and-toss,
Raced pigeons and greyhounds,
Played darts, dominoes, downed beer,
Sang, 'I'll take you home again, Kathleen.'

Pavements throbbed to the sound of clogs
In shifts, two thousand men,
At night the pit-gantry swung
To men's lamps like shooting stars.

Their lives lived to the pit they loved
Deep down, where there is still
Craftsmanship, comradeship.

One day I caught the bus
To wherever it was going.

Underground

Small voices shall be heard,
Though the voice may be a whisper
And the whisper a password,
Small voices shall be heard.

Small voices shall be heard,
Though driven underground
Still voices speak, undeterred.
Small voices shall be heard.

Small voices shall be heard
And gather strength, until
Momentum breaks the spell.
Small voices shall be heard.

Catland

Is there a God in catland
As they make their final purrs,
Is there a God in catland
For cats who say their prayers,
Mouser-friend
And house-friend
Is there a God at the end?

I reach out a hand to stroke you
Though I know you are not there,
I imagine I can hear you
As you purr inside your fur,
Mouser-friend
And house-friend,
Is there a God at the end?

Roll Call

John Berryman
Hart Crane
Cesare Pavese
Sylvia Plath
Etc. Etc.

(Poets, every one. Each committed suicide.)

Did they set out on a voyage and discover
That the world was not really round, but flat,
And stared into the frightening abyss, and slipped
Into the mania of the bewitched,
Urged towards the dark, like shoots towards the light.

Assembly Line

MondayTuesdayWednesdayThursdayFriday,
The assembly line of days,
Waiting for the end-product, Saturday,
Especially Saturday and Sunday.

Saturdays and Sundays are fun days
And much better than Mondays
Or Tuesdays and Wednesdays
And Thursdays and Fridays.

The Gunmen

A hurried knock at the door:
The hooded gunmen waited
With hate in their eyes
For the victim they had baited.

Before the door was opened
The victim asked, 'Who's there?'
'The police,' said the gunmen,
'Quick, there's a bomb scare.'

The victim, unsuspecting
Opened up the door,
Took the spray of bullets
And fell to the floor.

Home went the gunmen
And talked of blood and guns,
And with hatred in their eyes
Bred hatred in their sons.

The Meths' Drinker

The meths' drinker with the battle
For booze in a bottle,
Sees in every battle
A ship in every bottle,
For always the glass reads stormy
And the shelter of harbour
Is no comforter;
Reach, O reach me a bottle
To go into battle
In a ship, in a bottle,
Reach, reach,
To sail out to sea
Where my sea-legs feel at home.

Jack and Jill

Jack knew Jill was on the pill
And so they did as couples will
And Oh the bed it shook, until
Both Jack and Jill had their fill.
Then they both lay, very still.

Bumble - Bee

The bumble-bee
Is a fumble bee
Who likes to see
Things flowery,
Enters them devoutly
And devouringly,
Withdrawing bodily
All polleny.

1939

'No such undertaking has been received.'
And the earth shuddered
And the seas heaved
And the skies took a very deep breath
To make room for the dead.

Hiroshima

Things would never be the same again.
Or so we thought at the time. And then
Out of the rubble wild flowers grew,
Morning glory, panic grass and feverfew.

As My Father Lay Dying

At the time of the crocus
Purple and yellow and white,
You lay in your last winter
Of fast diminishing light.

Your family gathered round you
In the trappings of the ward,
And as we watched, time passed
At each drop of the saline drip.

In other beds were other heads
With glazed eyes and lolling tongues,
Waiting for the visitor,
Waiting for the light to fade.

Other heads? Just ornaments, you said,
And smiled your thinnest smile,
All, all the time to pass the time of day
But sagging heads slip into sleep.

Can't piss. Legs gone.
No homes. Redundant lungs.
Life's lovely flower gone to seed
Never to germinate again.

I watch time pass
At each drop of the saline drip
And reach back in reverie
To us as man and boy.

For me it was always summer,
The hawthorn lanes singing with yellow-hammers,
Throstles and blackbirds and linnets
And the lane had no end.

School: a girl with twin pigtails
And hair like silk,
Adorable Una McGurk
Just five years old.

Church: Our Father which art.
Sundays meant lucky-bags
And ice cream wafers
And sucked fingers dipped in sherbet.

Sleep: three to a bed,
One at the foot, two at the head.
When I woke, at each side of my face
A pair of my brothers' feet.

Give us this day: houses close to the pit
Pulled tight like a noose,
Around the houses, fields;
In the fields, slagheaps smelling of sulphur.

Lowered each day, the earth your roof and sky,
Dust and danger became part of you,
The disciplines of mines and men
Bred craftsmanship that shone like coal.

My mother, workhorse for the family,
Always kind and loving,
Thin as a scarecrow with asthma
She knew the meaning of breathing.

How to live on not enough money -
Gather blackberries for jam, glean peas,
Clean teeth with soot and salt,
Leave not a crumb nor a morsel.

The hurrying schoolboy strides over you
Asleep on the rug. A coal fire burns.
Still in pit clothes and coal-black face
Breakfast has washed your Al Jolson lips.

Our paths did not often cross.
When I was at home you worked.
When I was at school you slept.
Our meetings happened quite by chance.

Racing and your eye for a horse,
The white-gloved tic-tac, the parade,
The start, the shout, they're off. The thud
Of hooves raced with our beating hearts.

Greyhounds and their racing track.
The traps snap open to the hare
They'll never catch. Your favourites,
I remember, Redhow and Crossbow.

Age bent your back the pit could not break.
Retirement and your dearest loss.
To face the future alone
They presented you with a clock.

The pit was you.
Your blue scars were its veins.
Like Joyce's father you became
A praiser of your past.

Do you remember the doctor saying
That he'd keep an eye on you,
You asked would he mind keeping
Not one eye on you, but two.

I whizz down the big hill on a sledge.
Snowflakes get in my eyes.
No. It isn't snow. Each drop of the saline drip.
I see my own son at my own bedside.

Father, father,
I grip your hand in mine
And slip quietly away.

At the time of the crocus
Purple and yellow and white,
They lowered you for the last time
Where the darkness sheds no light.

To Absent Friends

Sir Osis of the liver
Cannot complain,
He was a bore at the bar
Time and time again.

Sir Flatulence, beg pardon,
Was sure he had an ulcer,
But arteries will harden
And a heart attack result, Sir.

My chain-smoking friend
Who loved the age of steam,
Thought life would never end
But that was just a dream.

Fred with his phobias
And slightly nervous tic,
Even with all of those
Still smiled at death's last trick.

Companions, every one.
A toast, as in the past.
Now I am left alone;
To Life: long may it last.

Gina

Suddenly,
Double-vision
Meant hospital and surgeons,
And Gina
A girl that I knew
Who loved horses,
Went for a ride on her horse
And galloped and galloped
And never came back.

Spinning

I marvel at the perfect embroidery
Of the spider's web, jewelled in dew,
Know that this flimsiest thread when dry
Will still be strong enough to catch a fly.

I, small fry, try spinning too.
Try to emulate the spider catch the fly
And hope the page before the ink runs dry
Will match the spider's spinning symmetry.

The Skylark

The skylark
Prepares for
Vertical take-off,
And balloons upwards
Buoyant with song
To a singing speck
In a search of sky.

Spent,
Descent
Is diminuendo,
When song
Stops,
Drops
Like a stone.

Miner With Silicosis

A hulk of a man in his dry-dock bed;
A cylinder the colour of coal
Piped oxygen to the mask around his head
Easing every difficult inhale,
I clumsily clashed two cylinders as I climbed the stairs
But he didn't stir.

The next day he was sitting up, on pillows propped,
Having kippers for tea. Look at this, he said.
I read some personal details, then stopped.
Read it. He wants you to see it, his wife said.
I looked from one to the other
And did as I was bid.

Headed on fine paper, the name of the Hospital Board.
We have found, through bronchitis, your chest deficient
(Having been examined by a medical team of three)
To a degree between 98 and 100 per cent.
I handed back the death warrant
And looked at the black cylinders.

Tha'll get nothing, not a penny, lass, he said,
Until they cut me open when I'm gone.
See that they do. Union fella'll see to it. Instead
Of bronchitis I know what they'll be finding then.
Having said that, he seemed relieved.
I know who I believed.

At The Head-Butting Ball

At the head-butting ball
There was a real free-for-all
With all holds barred and no clinching,
There were plenty of clashes
With deep, head-on gashes
As they butted, not one of them flinching.

It was hands behind backs
Into head-on attacks
And O were they having a ball,
There were no ifs, just butts,
With bleeding deep cuts
As everyone answered the call.

And the gals took a hand
And head-butted the band
For gals, too, now wear breeches,
They'll remember the night
At the head-butting fight
That had them all in stitches.

For all they had done
Was to go and have fun
And having fun cannot be bad,
For parental advice
Is all very nice
But mostly it's boring and sad.

But this time it was true
They were told what to do
For surely you've heard it said,
If you want to get on
Then dear daughter and son
For goodness sake, use your head.

Idling Speed

A car is parked, engine running,
Inside man in business suit,
Pale at gills, lack of sunning
But he doesn't give a hoot,
Knows that soon there will be fun in
Appointment with a prostitute.

Body Chemistry

There was chemistry
Between us,
Atoms of love
As we studied
Our molecular structure,
Elemental,
Exciting vibrations
In the discovering.

Cricket Grass-Widow

They seemed the perfect match.
But he took to watching willow,
She a cricket grass-widow
One of the faithful many,
But while he was away
She would take up with any
Man that took her fancy,
For she never missed a catch.

For You

You are my shelter
And my harbour, love,
You are my refuge
From the world without.

You are my progress
And my saviour, love,
You are my journey
On the map laid out.

You are calm waters
From the storm-tossed sea,
You are my rising
In a world of doubt.

You are my shelter
And my harbour, love,
You, my Lucifer,
Till the light goes out.

Weathers

The stuffed birds stare from the bare
Trees, waiting for the weather to get better.

Who would dare to question winter's
Long exclamation marks of icicles.

A thin, squared - off piece of string
Is frosted overnight into barbed wire.

Rain ices up. A skid of frost.
After black ice, black lace.

A dead bird that didn't make it.
That the cold winter left behind.

Now bullet - heads of daffodils
That soon will fire into flower.

Spring is birds singing
And buds feathering.

Upside down to a catkin clinging
A bumble-bee whilst nectaring.

Winds like autumn in contrary May
Blow away the blossom like confetti.

Now fires into power the sun
To set the heat - haze simmering.

And cricket can and shall survive
Through all the shades of green.

An artist painted autumn's leaves.
Dissatisfied, wiped the canvas clean.

The stuffed birds stare from the bare
Trees, waiting for the weather to get better.

Dry-Stone Walling

They divide or enclose
Fields, are most fitted
To fell landscape, sheep-tufted
Grazing, more permanent than

Hedgerows, offering resistance
They stand firm to the gales,
Will not break or bend
To let the wind through,

Can be, like hedgerows
A recluse for birds, mating,
Nesting; a search-warrant
For weasels, stoats, wanting

Succulent eggs; grow grimed
With age, time adds strength
For each accomplished stone
To withstand, endure centuries.

The enemy is frost, ice
The axe-man can
Fracture skeletal stones
Necessitating surgery.

Sun doesn't dazzle them,
They retain their composure
As the seasons change,
Encompassing land,

Firm, resolute in their structure,
They become lines on maps
And on deeds, set without mortar
And by man's hands made.

Habits

Old age creeps up on us,
Joints creak, lose fluidity,
The chest we slapped when young
'Me Tarzan' now thumps us,
We become more aware of ourselves.

We wheeze uphill, reach the summit, rest;
But plant no flag of victory:
Pop a tablet under your tongue
It isn't a bit like being young
But what is old age for?

It is not death I fear, but age.
Gracefully I look back and see below
The young, deaf to old age, with ear-muffs on
Listening to their endless songs of love.

To Stanley Horner

I called the other day
But you weren't in,
And you had left
No forwarding address,
Most unlike you,
Stanley.

I want you to know wherever you are
That things are progressing just as you
Would have wished. The factory is producing,
The salesmen are out selling,
And the sales graph is upwards
And rising.

Simon, your son, sits in your chair.
The directors hold regular meetings,
People still matter most and are believed in,
And the profits are ploughed back
Manuring the future
As you and Dorothy always did.

That famous Pickles' ointment in a tin
For corns and hard skin,
Filled at first by Dorothy
And sold by you
Two dozen on a card displayed
To chemists countrywide.

A one-line firm. A man-and-wife team.
If you hadn't believed in yourselves
The trough of despair awaited;
You found your friends through your fears.
You had a head for feet -
Now it's assets in the balance - sheet.

And to start after fifty
When most are unwinding downhill,
You cranked the engine
And set off each week, your Dormobile
Stuffed with Pickles' tins
And books to read at night,

Hazlitt, Johnson (Sam),
The Bard, The Bible;
At day's end your Dormobile
Was your hotel
Parked in any convenient spot,
A lay-by or a parking lot.

There you could read and talk to yourself,
Feel the words rolling like wine
On your tongue, with no one to think
You might be going off your head,
Not learning for the sake of earning
But learning for the love of learning.

You built widthways,
And as the years advanced
More orders brought more success,
More success, more people
Gladly adding
More bricks to your foundation-stone.

Not that you sold just for selling's sake
But more for the art of it,
The thrill of it,
The thing in itself,
As all life pervades
To everything that persuades.

You of the generous gesture
And the full glass,
Warm conversation flowed
Until words were tipsy,
Business, books, whirled
In the whisk of the world.

Shock. The suddeness of it.
A stroke. Speech locked within you.
Touch and go. Ebb and flow.
A wheelchair for your brisk walk.
Life's allotted span
Sometimes makes a mockery of man.

You wanted desperately to speak
But the brain had forgotten its lines.
You could have written a treatise
On black despair,
Trying to learn ABC again
But it wasn't to be again.

If I had the gift
To perform miracles,
I would have given you back
The power of speech,
Would have uncramped your hands
To hold a glass, a pen again.

Donnish looking, my professor,
(Stop pissing up my back, you said.)
Blue eyes and white clouds
Blue skies and white hair,
You could have preached to the unconverted,
Spread quotations as easily as butter on bread.

I know that we must all join
The everlasting procession,
But Stanley, wherever you are,
Wherever you are, Stanley,
Make it rain, make it rain,
And make it rain - whisky.

Man's best friend

A dog is man's best friend, no doubt
And needs its daily walkabout
To do its bit, but all of my friends
Think dogs should be muzzled – at both ends.

The Double Glazier's Love Song

As I was double glazing early
I saw you still in bed quite clearly
Through the glass and very nearly
Crept into you. You obviously didn't hear me.
I could have clutched you passionately near me.
You would have been but putty in my hands.

Poet fishing

I cast the line into the pool of wait,
Plumb the depths, feed the swim with bait,
Stare at the mirror surface.

Let an image be made. The quill float
Dips to the murks of ink,
Fishermen are statues on the bank.

Is this pool fishless?
Wait. Cast again. Cast again and wait.
Feed the swim. Feed the swim with bait.

I wait. I wait. I wait. I wait. I wait.
The quill drills to a point behind my eyes.
Time is away and everything besides.

The ripple rings of promise reach boiling point.
The plunge of the pool is racing line away.
I play the fish till it's silver in my hands.

A letter to my father

Pit Closures

Dad. The hole you went down has been filled in.
Grassed over. A mining village has died.
The pit headgear, the whoosh of work, all gone.
There are idle hands. Grass grows. Dignified.

You see, Dad, coal is a dirty fuel.
An MP said so. His name, Heseltine.
In a statement, and the House was full
He said price had forced the pits into decline.

There are but a dozen or so pits left now
And soon there won't be any left at all,
No gear to wear, no fear to fear, and no
Cages for the descent just like free fall.

Dad. We still come home to a real coal fire,
It burns just like one, and powered by gas
The coals go rosy glow and will forever
For this fire's always laid and leaves no ash.

Golfer: Fred Beaumont

On the tee: Fred Beaumont,
No longer long
Or quite so strong,
Under a frail sky
The fairways lie,
Fairways were
Made for him,
Always straight
And always true
He never did deviate.
Once on the green
He would invite
You to putt first,
Such a good chip-and-putt man;
The final hole approaches, Fred,
I hear them call your name:
You're on the fairway, Fred,
For your second, take a wood,
Well struck, Fred, the shot is good,
Fred, it's heading for the pin,
Fred, Fred, it's going in.

Snapdragon

Pinch its side
With forefinger and thumb
And it goes open-mouthed,
Such voluptuousness
The bee can't resist
And ravenous
Enters,
Totally
Enveloped.

To Be A Condom

O it's swell to be a condom
To feel needed just by someone,
In a packet
In a pocket
Near where the heart beats like a gong.

You can tell when love is coming
Like the tide roaring in,
Wave on wave on wave of loving
Surely loving can't be sin,
If it is, include me in.

O the love play and the foreplay
And the hoped for more and more play
Till it reaches a crescendo:
Hold it there and never end. O
Love is music; music, love.

Spent. I'm flushed away. The sea
Sometimes accommodates me,
Still the tide roaring in
Wave on wave on wave of loving,
Love's a very busy thing.

Though I've lived life in a packet
And been in the protection racket
Yet I'm no criminal. I've
Neither added to, nor taken life.
Now just flotsam, I survive.

A Russian Blue Cat

A Russian Blue cat
Is a just-for-you cat,
It doesn't stray
Or go far away.

And for a cat that
Is good. Cars go squat.
And that can be that
For any cat.

A cat needs more
Than nine lives now.
Car drivers need
Many more than that.

Bottle Bank

There's a bottle bank
At the bottom of our garden
That takes bottles mostly coloured green,
For I am a secret drinker
One of the great unseen,

But always a neighbourly neighbour
For what would the neighbours think
If they knew their next-door neighbour
Was one who took a secret drink,
So I've had a silencer fitted

Now the bottles slide quietly in,
With not so much noise as a tonic
Hissing into a neat glass of gin,
And that keeps the green peace between us
And with me, a great peace, within.

Song Of The Air

O we are seven miles up and all boozed up
And earth is seven below,
But we don't care, we are high in the air
Making the party go.

Make mine a triple, that's my tipple
Once earth is seven below,
And would you like ice, that would be nice,
In the land of the Eskimo.

For outside it's snow, the cloud below
Just like the land of the Eskimo,
Sometimes you see through a patch of blue
Where the sea is seven below.

Like you and me, the crinkled sea
Goes on its ageing way,
A tiny boat like an arrow afloat
Points to its destiny.

O we are seven miles up and all boozed up
And earth is seven below,
But we don't care, we are high in the air
Making the party go.

Then the captain said, turbulence ahead
Fasten your seat-belts, please,
We are arrowing to a place he knew
Far beyond the ageing seas.

Summer Hummer

Bees busy with flowers -
Life's full of honey,
Slugs and greenfly
Are minus money,
Spray the greenfly -
Get rid of slugs -
But don't forget
Bees give us a buzz.

Air

My mother had fortitude beyond compare
Battling for breath as each spasm seized her.

She gasped for air. Grasped at air. She needed it.
Great lungfuls. Great big begging-bowls of it.

Asthma they called it. It never left her.
Does air exist? You can't see it. Is it there?

Each night the slow, Everest climb of stairs
From base-camp to peak till the bed was hers.

There, propped on pillows, five, six, seven steep
In a sitting position she wheezed to sleep.

If she went silent I crept into her
And looked for movement that life was still with her.

The delicate air. The Oh! so delicate air,
That we who breathe never know it's there.

Mortgaged

Yes, my lovey-dovey, I'll take you
To be my husband and I'll stay true.

When you wake up one morning in bed
You find you've a mortgage over your head.

Then you get your yearly statement.
Add the interest, deduct payments, and where are you?

Back where you started. It doesn't seem fair.
And both working. Then there's wear and tear.

The bed becomes an object - at a price.
It won't be paid for with confetti and rice.

Bricks and mortar changes everything.
The bed is beginning to lose its spring.

Love Song

Opposites attract, they say
Just like magnets do,
The first time I set eyes on you
I knew that it was true,
Now you are so close to me
And I'm so close to you.

Romeo and Juliet,
Anthony and Cleopatra,
They were pretty good at it
And many who came after,
You and me, why shouldn't we
Sublime into history?

Bearings

Where has God gone?
Where are the spires?
Has evil won?
Where are the choirs?

Do they still kneel
Father and son,
Lay down a keel
To build upon,

Proudly let slip
Ship into sea,
With fellowship
Say follow me?

Where do we go
Once we leave here?
How shall we know
What course to steer?

Scholarship Lads

We were scholarship lads
Above ground, playing around
Whilst our dads underground
Worked the burrowing seams,
There were to be no knee-pads
For us, but dreams, dreams, dreams.

They coughed it up for us
So that we could be free
For whatever would be
And we each took our chance,
Then we went our separate ways
To the Earth's four corners.

Cricket Comes

At the sea's edge, where the land begins,
On smooth, sea-drained sand
A father is bowling to his son;
Family and friends field
And on the breeze the game starts to swing.

Cricket comes, collects its followers
And carries them through the summer,
And omens hoped the game may bring
No one can tell until it ends, or
The spin of a coin and how it lands.

Cricket needs its variations;
Its ups and downs, its fast and slows,
As this land flows in humps and hollows
Towards the horizon's boundary
Where the Pennines meet the sky.

On a scattering of grounds
Play sets the summer free;
It is as if someone above had sprinkled seed
And where it fell, cricket grounds grew,
To make each summer fresh, each summer, new.

Cricket Calypso

England v West Indies 1980

The 1980 calypso
Is very fast with not much slow.

One, two, three, four, here we go
Very fast with not much slow.

Fast bowlers come in pairs, they say,
But two pairs stacked to fill the day –
Fours to a full house watch them play
Aces in hand and the chocks away.

One, two, three, four, ho, ho, ho,
Holding, Garner, Croft and Co.

The crowd is swaying
To and fro
To beer cans playing
Calypso,
Lovely cricket calypso.

One, two, three, four in full flow,
Very fast with not much slow.

English batsmen sleep lightly, O
They know the night will quickly go,
And morning bowls them fast, not slow,
Batsmen come and batsmen go.

One, two, three, four, ho, ho ,ho,
Very fast with not much slow.

Who would like to face them? O
So very fast with not much slow,
Ghosts from the past cry quickly, No!
Even Hornby and Barlow.

One, two, three, four, there they go
Very fast with not much slow.

The crowd is swaying
To and fro
To beer cans playing
Calypso,
Lovely cricket calypso.

Sonny Ramadhin

On a small ground, in a small town
In Lancashire, a small man,
Ramadhin, is bowling; his arm comes over
Making disbelievers believe in magic.

Time was he could make cities move,
Crowds converged, with applause ringed him;
Magic enough, his shirt sleeve flapping,
England, no wicket could read him.

Hutton said: 'Treat him like a great man,
Play him down the line.'
Play him down the line into
The passages of time

To Sir Len Hutton

There was no violence in him, rather
The quiet mathematician
Given over to geometrics
And the study of angles,
Arcs,
Perimeters and perpendiculars,
Curves and dividing lines,
But rarely, rarely
The parabola.

And the mystery of it all
Was the mastery of it all.

J. H. Wardle

A slow left-armer
And quite a charmer,
Johnny Wardle
Didn't dawdle,
Though they don't play
He bowled Chinamen,
And on his day
He'd clown away;
A drive, waist high
Past him would fly
Like a rocket
To the boundary;
He'd turn, look that way,
But the ball was pouched –
Safely in his pocket.

Openers

Openers should be there to stay,
At least until the close of play.

And should a ball begin to shoot –
Take heart, Geoff Boycott's taking root.

An early yorker, soon dug out
By Geoffrey Boycott, digging in.

Fast bowlers, full of fire, perspire
And bowl at Geoffrey, then retire.

From early on, the hook shot
Is not one for Geoffrey Boycott.

But look, there's a lovely square cut –
Favourite shot of Geoffrey Boycott,

A shot all along the ground
Pleasing to eye with pleasant sound.

Now comes convoluting spin
Testing technique and discipline.

Openers should be there to stay,
At least until the close of play.

On many a worldly cricket square
Geoffrey Boycott, dedicated there.

England v Australia

Headingley, Monday, July 20th 1981

TRIBUTE TO IAN BOTHAM

Back from zero
To a hero;
Six-wicket-taker,
Fifty-maker,
England, following on
And the match nearly gone,
Mighty Ian Botham
Strides towards the crisis,
Peppers fours to applause –
Keeps as cool as ice is,
Along with Graham Dilley
Lifts the whole of Headingley,
Nineteen fours and a six
Add to his century mix,
Taken all in eighty-seven balls
Oh the rises and the falls,
As the score goes up and up
Some recall the famous Jessop.

Back from zero
To a hero,
Mighty Ian Botham.

F. S. Trueman

With that lovely action that fast bowlers envy,
But not batsmen facing the full fury of Fiery,
To his curved run-in the slips crouch easily
Waiting eagerly for the snick fast coming their way.

And if not, stopped in his track, a glare and a stare
At the batsman, then the walk back, fingers combing hair,
Now, ball in hand, polishing the flannelled groin red,
Turning again, the batsman wondering what lies ahead.

Between overs, crouched at short-leg, a flute of sweet grass
In his mouth plays the tune 'None shall pass'
To his quicksilver pick-up. About batting, what sticks
In the mind is the crowd always wanting a six.

Authority, set there, like a mountain to climb,
With vitriol and humour, legend in his lifetime,
But that lovely action that fast bowlers envy,
With his own stamp of authority, sealed on memory.

Joel Garner

Joel Garner is six foot eight
And that's a height to contemplate.

With those high handed deliveries
He's well equipped to clinch a series.

He doesn't bounce them down the pitch
But bowls a length and strikes it rich.

One can imagine that the angle
Has many batsmen in a tangle.

Did they first invent the visor
To counteract the Joel riser?

A batsman in full-suited armour
Is best equipped for Joel Garner.

Batsmen at the other end
Feel at least they'll face a friend.

Viv Richards

He is a magnum of champagne, popping;
Now see the bubbles freely rise,
From the start there is no stopping
The urgent flow of boundaries.

Open up another bottle!
This cricket is to celebrate,
Frenzied bowlers locked in battle
And Viv with runs to dissipate.

Let us not compare vintages
Though it's for vintages we live,
Certain years yield advantages
Just raise your glasses, here's to Viv.

Making a Cricket Bat

(With gratitude to Colin Easter and Rowland Baum of Crown Sports, Dewsbury, Yorkshire)

Take a piece of wood, but willow,
And choose with care the finest edge
That only craftsmen will allow,
And with that cleft shaped like a wedge,

Plane the face, then to laws comply,
Cutting to length and cut to width,
Bevel the back wood, then compress;
The blade now half the weight it was.

Take certain lengths of Manau cane,
Glue strips of rubber in between,
Round off the cane, bind all again,
Serve shape until a handle's seen.

The handle arrows into the V.
No nail, no pin and no device
Other than fitting perfectly
Along with glue secures the splice.

The handle clamped, with drawknife peel
With sweeping cuts pare blade away,
And expert hands with eye and feel
Match experts on the field of play.

Hook out the shoulders, sand the blade,
The handle twined, with rubber rolled,
Add to the blade the make and grade
So proudly played throughout the world.

See how the years of age in lines
Run down the shining blade like veins,
Look how these craftsmen shape their lives
With rows of bats, ready for runs.

Keith Miller

As a bowler,
One of a pair,
A fast pair –
None deadlier,
Lindwall and Miller.

Keith Miller,
Debonair,
Devil-may-care,
Might turn in his run anywhere.

But beware
Of devil-may-care,
Not couldn't care less
But a terrier.

He loved the tight
Corner, like a figher pilot
In a dogfight;
Once in his sight
He'd press the button.
Ask Hutton.

The Umpire

As a player, he would
Have liked to be
First in and last out,
Now he's first out
And last in,
What a turnabout
Is umpiring.

Retiring
From the game left a gap
Like an ache; what he knew best
He knew best what to do,
To give back to the game
What the game had given him:
So to umpiring.

Now he occupies the field of play
All day, has a player's instinct
For the game, the judge's impartiality,
And summers are green again,
He can mix with crowds unrecognised
But knows that in the first-class games
TV can freeze a frame
And show to millions
The human frailties of the game.

Elegy for Jim Laker

*Incomparable Surrey and England off-spinner,
died April 23rd 1986*

On Tuesday, May 6th, his ashes were scattered on The Oval. Surrey said in a statement: 'At the request of Mrs Lily Laker and in accordance with Jim Laker's wishes, his ashes were scattered on The Oval today by Micky Stewart, the Surrey director of cricket.'

Let them on light breezes blow
Scattered now without a sound
On this hallowed Oval ground.

Let them on light breezes blow,
Let them settle where they will,
Let them settle with his skill.

Let them on light breezes blow,
Let them curve and flight in air
Just like his artistry there.

Let them on light breezes blow,
Let them settle where they will,
Let them settle with his skill,
Let them settle, and be still.

Brian Statham

If you drew a line wicket to wicket
It was as if he'd drilled it,
Fast bowling and make the batsman play –
That's how he willed it.

Bowling against the wind or with it,
Unspectacular, but nagging like a pain,
Always a team man, often his partner
Because of him, showed the better gain.

Not seeking headlines, just bowling to batsmen
With vigour, he didn't seem to hate them,
Through and through, straight and true,
For county and country, Brian Statham.

Garry Sobers

As a youngster may notch
His name on a tree
Just to show that he's been there,
Never imagining
That in later years
As the tree grows in girth
So might his name
Enlarge into fame,
Such was Garry Sobers
Of Barbados and the West Indies.
From playing lilliputian cricket
He became a colossus,
Spreading himself across the pages of the day,
Spreading himself across the pages of forever.

There you'll find him
In the wonders of Wisden,
Centuries in Tests,
Propping up Bradman,
Six sixes
In a six-ball over,
365 not-out
In a Test in Jamaica.
At fielding
You'll find him at slip
Or leg slip,
Always in the game
In the game closing in,
110 catches
In 93 Test matches.

How would you like
In your side
A three-in-one bowler,
Is that possible?
Fast left-arm for starters
Good enough to test most openers,
Then on into the afternoon and evening
With spin and spin and spin again;
Left-arm wrist spin, left-arm finger spin,
Then slip the giggly-googly in;
One of that faith
With a belief in attacking,
The earth spins on its axis
With Sobers pivotal –
And how was that!

Frank Tyson at Sydney, 1954

There was no need to time him
Either by stopwatch
Or electronically,
Evans and the slips took steps farther back,
For the batsmen in the pavilion
The message spread like a bushfire,
The Hill went silent;
This was speed
And a speed seldom seen,
Tyson bowling
And fully in possession of himself.

Nurtured
In Middleton,
The raw recruit rapped
Hutton on the pads at Redcar,
The hurt mapped in the mind
A letter to higher authority
Saying a fast bowler was thundering;
The lightning struck at Sydney.

Back home,
Rubbed in the dust
At Northampton,
The pitch with a sign
NOT WANTED. RESERVED
MOSTLY FOR SPINNERS:
The pulse for the quick fast fading,
He went like Larwood before him
To live and work where the fire was,
Down under.

Brian Close

Not the loud fanfare of trumpets
That leads to the boxing ring,
But the long, slow, quiet walk
To the square for cricketing,
But in the make-up of the man
There was the selfsame thing.

To give an inch? Flinch from line?
Or throw the towel in?
With firmness of jaw,
Right hand or southpaw,
He'd lose his teeth before withdraw,
Which is the cardinal sin.

For in the make-up of the man
The square was a boxing ring.

Jamaica, Jamacia

The first Test, West Indies v England at Sabina Park, February 23rd, 24th & 25th 1986

FOR FRANK HOWSE

Jamaica, Jamaica
Island in the sun,
Welcomes everyone,
Welcomes everyone,
Jamaica, Jamacia,
Island full of fun,
Welcomes everyone
Ev..en Eng..lish..men.

Jamaica, Jamaica,
Island in the sun,
Welcomes everyone,
And so full of fun,
Get used to relaxing pace
That's what the brochure says,
Tell that to the Englishmen
Who have four fast to face.

Jamaica, Jamaica, O!
To Sabina Park we go
Where the kites are flying high
And there are vultures in the sky
And I know the reason why –
Though you call your vulture a crow,
They are waiting for the Englishmen to face
Your four bowlers full of fearsome pace.

England batting, without Gatting,
Now there's a body blow,
The England openers seem in touch
Tim Robinson and Graham Gooch,
But some balls are bouncing high
And some are shooting low,
They are firing missiles from a gun –
Holding, Garner, Marshall, Patterson.

The openers last an uneasy hour.
Then Robinson goes after scoring six
Caught at slip by Gordon Greenidge,
Next comes the slim captain, David Gower,
And with Gower power hits a six
But don't applaud it's over slips,
Then he makes one more boundary score
But again it's high over slips for four.

This is no English pudding of a pitch
But baked hard by the sun to strike it rich,
Done to a turn, it's just made for pace
And Windies have four fearsome fast to face,
Gower leaves; Smith makes one lonely run,
One more than his second innings – none;
Lamb is the next for this cricket cauldron,
Holding, Garner, Marshall, Patterson.

Lunch. 3 wickets down. Then a lifter
For Gooch, caught gully for fifty-one.
Now in comes mightly Ian Botham
But bats restrained as if chained,
Soon Marshall round-the-wicket goes
And all can see, even the crows,
The hook-trap set, Patterson the bait,
And Botham bites, he just can't wait.

Look at Willey, looking silly
With that two-eyed stance. Man
Why do you bat like that, chest-on,
How stroke de ball to de boundaree ?
Man! You make us laugh. You a clown ?
Listen to laughing all roun de ground.
See. Dujon is a good glove man
And catches Willey out for none.

When Columbus sailed the ocean blue
Did he guess they would bowl as few
As 68 overs in a full day's play.
That must be a record in a way.
For 39 runs they took England's last five
But the team's still standing, all alive,
Though they are firing missiles from a gun,
Holding, Garner, Marshall, Patterson.

Is this a one-day match?
Have they got a plane to catch?
Greenidge and Haynes are in clover
Scoring runs at six an over.
A Red Stripe. To the boundary, of course,
Stag bitter man, on ice, on ice,
They are giving us the run-around
And our faces in the stand are beetroot-red.

The first day's play has ended.
The Blue Mountain range is far away.
We walk back, the two of us,
To our hotel, The Pegasus,
Wary of manholes with no covers on.
Jamaica, with your sense of fun
You've left the tops off many a one,
Holes for the English to fall into?

The game resuming and the sun is fuming.
One, two, three wickets down, then four,
But they've already passed England's score.
Gomes adds a steadying fifty-six
And there's 58 from Gordon Greenidge,
Carlyle Best's first scoring stroke is six,
One for Wisden's Test statistics;
Dujon adds a priceless 54.

Ellison for England took 5 for 78.
The others far too few for far too many.
Six lbw's went England's way
The finger pointing to fair play,
But England's 159, Windies 307,
Leaves us to score 148 to level.
The vultures will not go away,
They know the exact state of play.

Get used to relaxing pace
That's what the brochure says,
But what the vultures ask
Is, will this match last three days?
Jamaica with your sense of fun
They know this pitch is a tricky one,
They are waiting for the Englishmen to face
Your four bowlers full of fearsome pace.

They are weaving and ducking
And ducking and weaving,
Helmeted batsmen fighing a war,
The ball a bullet, what are bullets for,
They are going and coming
And between lulls running
Over the top, facing missiles from a gun,
Holding, Garner, Marshall, Patterson.

Two ducks for openers. Prey for the vultures?
The innings is hurrying towards its end
But one man adds a stiffening,
That man they laughed at, Peter Willey,
Has 71 reasons for saying so.
His beard hides the sternest chin,
They shall not laugh at me again,
Remember me. And Barrington.

Who wants a spinner on this uneven track?
Perm any two from four for a fast attack.
West Indies just has that fearsome four
And waiting in the wings are many more.
At the fall of every wicket touch the flesh,
At the fall of every wicket leap afresh.
England crumble, all out one/five/two,
Windies scoring five, and that will do.

The first Test match has ended.
The pitch halfway down is pitted red.
The vultures have had their fill
And have soared over the hill,
Now Sabina Park is still
So very still,
Jamaica, you have had your fun.
Well done, Windies, Well done. Well done.

England v The West Indies 1988

One, two, three, four, here we go again,
Marshall, Ambrose, Walsh and Benjamin.

One, two, three, four in full flow,
Very fast with not much slow.

One, two, three, four, full speed ahead
At the English batsmen, all helmeted.

England, three Tests down. Just one to go.
One, two, three, four, ho, ho, ho.

Perm any two from four. Here we go again;
Marshall, Ambrose, Walsh and Benjamin.

Where do they find them? On the sea shore,
Playing at softball and there's many more.

They are not softies. Put a hard ball in their hand
Playing for their country against England

And it's one, two, three, four in full flow,
Very fast with not much slow.

One, two, three, four, here we go again,
Marshall, Ambrose, Walsh and Benjamin.

Mike Brearley

In the field, unfussy,
Not a loud, slap-on-the-back man,
He would be just as much at home
Wearing cap and gown,
Crossing quadrangles
To quiet rooms,
Pondering on variables, options,
As he is here, now, on this cricket field,
Quick and alert
Behind the calm exterior,
The slight gesture for a field change,
A raised eyebrow even;
Experience shows like his grey hair,
The whole orchestra aware of his conducting presence.

Not, as a batsman, of the highest class,
But the first to wear a head-protector;
A wise move that for a wise head,
For as captain, players pulled for him
And many a match, seemingly lost
Cost the opposition dearly;
As Rodney Hogg said,
You have a degree in People, Mike Brearley.

Death of John Arlott

Alderney, December 14th 1991

The waves hold back from Alderney's shore,
The gulls keep their silent vigil overhead,
The umpires confer about the light,
The microphones will say: John Arlott is dead.

Now claret gathers more dust in his cellar
And all the vintage years have gone;
He took his best bottles with him
For he drank deep in everything he'd done.

The waves resume their commentaries.
The gulls begin to cry again.
In easeful glide, their fly-past salutes
Cricket's voice and cricket's pen.

He is here. Pen poised above paper,
Swirling the rhythms around his tongue,
His poems are wanting to be read
And his hymns are waiting to be sung.

He is here. Microphone at hand,
His unique voice in the sound archives
Getting the message of cricket
So lovingly across the waves.

Cricket at Upton

(For Leonard Parkin)

The pitch a patch of green; close by, slagheaps;
The strip between two cart ruts; our four strong
Gang of grammar school lads took measured leaps,
Twenty two, twelve-year-old-boy-strides long .

Wickets were coats hung like scarecrows on sticks,
No pads, no gloves, no protection at all,
The bowler hurling what looked like round red bricks -
It hurt when you were hit with that corky ball.

There were no helmets then; they were for dads
Who worked the burrowing seams of coal
With half a mile of earth above their heads,
Whilst we played cricket and took turns to bowl.

Lucky for us not asked to follow on;
Free to choose whatever we wished to be,
You, Len, took up the pen and microphone
And worked for BBC and ITV.

You reported the death of Kennedy,
Watched wars whilst bullets whizzed before your eyes,
Interviewed statesmen, spacemen, on TV
And never showed a trace of butterflies.

Cricket Calendar

January, and fresh hopes rise
Like bubbles in champagne,
To head the averages
Or be the team captain.

Boys blow hands to keep warm
It's frosty and snowing,
And soon with practised arm
They are snowball throwing.

Pad up into the March nets
And practise the game indoors,
Though not the same when it's
Played on hard wooden floors.

April, and spring is here
And life's worth living, lads,
Get out your cricket gear
And buckle on your pads.

There's a nip in the air
And some zip off the pitch,
And batsmen suspect there
May be a tricky patch.

The game as it should be
June sunshine the setting,
Crowd and cricketers happy
And runs for the getting.

July scoreboard threatening
Imminent disaster
Finds a hero emerging -
A minnow to a master.

This August game can crowd
An hour into a minute,
And silences grow loud
To all the glories in it.

Sponsored knock-out finals
With many fours and threes,
September festivals
With sea air and marquees.

October. With regret
We put away our gear,
We were just getting set
But leaves say autumn's here.

November, with dinners,
Talk, a tankard and toasts:
To the game, its winners;
All visitors and hosts.

December could bring
Books for your stocking,
Giving joy to those of us
Cricket crackers at Christmas.

Freddie Flintoff

You can't get enough
Of Freddie Flintoff,
He scatters sixes
Amongst the sexes.

He takes catches
That win matches,
Catches sublime
Caught in real time.

He peppers with flak
The ace in the pack,
And bowls the best
Not just nine, ten, jack.

He fills the screen
Like W.G.,
Up with the best
There's ever been.

Superhuman —
He's worth two men.

A Prayer for Cricketers

In my work and in my play
Be part of me.

In my life, in every way
Be part of me.

In my living, every day
Be part of me.

All my life, till close of play
Be part of me.

Millennium Hymn and Tune

Now we await the midnight hour
On this very special day,
And the bells peal out their power
Calling us to kneel and pray,
For You were born that we might live –
And You taught us life is love,
And though betrayed You could forgive –
In Your hands You held a dove.

The good news spread about Your birth
Across continent and sea,
Your seed took root in the rich earth
And it grew a family tree,
Where there was darkness You brought light,
Life has meaning - Wise Men knew
The star that guided them that night
Was someone uniquely You.

Under the dome that is the sky
In Your house our praise we sing,
As each succeeding day goes by
In Your house our prayers we bring,
When T.V. screens show those in need
Help us put the wrongs to right,
Where lands breed tyranny and greed
Free the chains of those bound tight.

Who could imagine man in space?
Launch pad rocket fuels burn
And lift-off fires the human race
With belief in their return.
Man on the moon. In God we trust.
Man is a creator, too,
Earth footprints in the lunar dust –
Guide us in the ways of You.

Now let there celebrations be –
Twenty centuries ago
With miracles in Galilee
Your life set the world aglow,
Millennium, Millennium,
Welcome the Millennium,
Praise Him who came for those to come –
Welcome the Millennium.

Published by OAK PRESS (Bradford) Ltd.
113 Station Lane
Bradford
BD11 2BX